TRAVELS

A Poetic Journey

James (Jim) McManus 2023

Travels – A Poetic Journey is in the public domain. All original additions, including illustrations and chapter summaries, are copyright © [2023] by James (Jim) McManus and may not be reproduced in any form without written permission from the publisher or author, except as permitted by U.S. copyright law.

ISBN:979-8365694279

Dear Hannah,

We travel, some of us forever, to seek our lives, our souls, to discover who we are. More importantly, who we were.

I hope you enjoy the read dear friend!

James (Jim) McManus
October 2023

"We travel, some of us forever, to seek other states, lives, and souls."

- anaïs nin

DEDICATION

This book of poetry is written in memory of a Father. His constant love, mentorship, and friendship underscored my respect and admiration for him. Without his presence in my life, these words of prose would never have been possible.

"I believe that what we become depends on what our fathers teach us at odd moments when they aren't trying to teach us. Little scraps of wisdom form us."

—— Umberto Eco

CONTENTS

Dedication

Forward

Introduction

The Journey

Those Love Things

Just Poetry

Acknowledgments

About the Author

FORWARD

If I could only use one word to describe Jim's writing, it would be heartfelt. It is such an honor to write this forward for Travels: A Poetic Journey where Jim takes us on a voyage through darkness, sweet sadness, crushing love, mental anguish, hope and healing. Jim's reflections, quotes and display of artist renditions further enhances this stunning collection of poetry.

Travels is an authentic and raw creative effort that gives the reader a nudge to explore their own experiences and emotions. Jim is certainly no ordinary writer – he relays his personal experiences in a soulful way that respects how his past has influenced the man he is today. And diving into his pain makes the reader fully feel as well. My thought upon reading Jim's beautiful book was this: How can we regret Jim's past when it has led him to the writing he finds such solace in and shares with us today?

Fazila Moosa – Author of Words of Healing Letter by Letter

INTRODUCTION

In moments of reflection, I often recall how my early years were altered through addiction. As I ripened, I watched a spirit diminish from the afflictions deep inside. It carried with it a heavy burden, inciting my soul endlessly for peace, a peace that never came.

Looking back with a tender sadness, I can now understand it was a time of darkness and euphoria.

These words are a way of forgiving myself for not appreciating the difficulties of life that can break a young man's spirit.

I have come to those dark memories with a perspective that, in those moments, I was naive, not realizing there would be more to me than yesterday.

But now it's in these words that I'm able to acknowledge it, listen to its truth, and speak it back to you as poetry; it's a form of acceptance - it's this tender sadness that gives birth to a new consciousness, welcoming peace that finally has arrived.

These words of poetry are reflections of my travels throughout life. They represent a lifetime of joy, suffering, pain, grief, anxieties, those love things, and moments of peaceful solitude. They are my way of expunging those introspections I've carried for too long. I hope you enjoy these words about poetic complexity of one man's travels through life.

THE JOURNEY

"Poetry is just the evidence of life.
If your life is burning well, poetry is just the ash."

—— Leonard Cohen

Artist Credits - © Donna M. Magsoling
Donna Marie @dawnnnaaaa

"I will be stronger than my sadness."

—— Jasmine Warga

TRAVELS

(Sea of Misery)

On a dreary night, with a weak and weary body, she couldn't hear a sound except for a painful heartbeat—it was fast and steady as she goes

Drifting along into the dark loneliness, surrounded by a nothingness consuming happiness, it was as if I was severed into an opaque world, absorbing every spirited thought as if it might be my last

Uttering agonizing words, needing to escape this painful world - imploring the sea, thirsting for its waves surging only for me - scripting, every syllable strung into jagged snares of poetry, flowing from my tongue as I drown into the cruel reality of my tormented soul

Cast away into a starry darkness looming on the horizon completely alone, adrift with reflections on a vast sea of misery from which there is no return – these travels of mine into that dark loneliness

Steady as she goes

- Writer's Thoughts -

This poetry was inspired and written by the Artist of the Book cover Donna M. Magsoling, and edited by the Author.

Ms. Magsoling has made significant contributions to this project, from genesis to artistic design, to providing written poems. It is only fitting that she be given the honor of the opening poem.

Artist Credits - © Eskander Dawani
@iskander.dawani

"This world that I live in is empty and cold;
the loneliness cuts me and tortures my soul."

—— Waylon Jennings

LAST AGONY

Ink transfused through my veins, with feelings of obsession as those words of poetry bleed with the fervor of a last agony

Speaking in tongues, with lyrics telling me there's no peace inside anymore, just dark empty corridors on the way to a lonely cold purgatory

Those anxieties never seem to fade, all I got now are these dark words of poetry bleeding through the veins of a tormented soul

Waiting for sanity to slip away, feeling like it just isn't worth it anymore; with a need to leave this emotional persecution of mine behind

Seems like this poetry is begging for that one last agony to come and harvest this tired old soul of mine

Thinking it's just time anyhow

- Writer's Thoughts -

I wrote this piece during a time of great emotional distress. The feelings of despair consumed my sense of reality. Closed off in my own lonely world all I wanted was for that last agony to come harvest this weary tired old soul of mine.

Two years ago, I started a path of healing through poetry. It's only now I feel comfortable sharing my pain with the ones closest to me. They never knew that side of my fragility, they just never knew that part of me.

Artist Credits – © Yeimei Wangsa
@ymei_iem

"Sometimes poetry--words--give us a small, lovely look at ourselves. And sometimes that is enough."

—— Patricia MacLachlan

A GLIMPSE OF ME

I was once a genius in my dreams; I've always had some sort of adversity; I have a heart that aches as if it doesn't belong to me; I always feel a sense of undignified anxiety

Everything seems to be wilting inside me; even that knowledge I once craved is now just a distant memory

Every pondered deliberation feels the weight of my unintended scrutiny; knowing there's so much more unwritten poetry to be composed, I'm just out here speculating if my words are surrendering a glimpse of who used to reside inside me

- Writer's Thoughts -

Having lived as if each day would be my last, I write about those fading memories of yesterday and not about who I am today.

Artist Credits - © Viktoriya (Vicky) Golbraykh
@vickyssketchbook

"How can I begin anything new with all of yesterday in me?"

—— Leonard Cohen

THE PROBLEM WITH POETRY

The problem with poetry is it encourages the writing of more poetry

I'm always wondering how it will ever end. Will the day finally arrive when we have described everything in the world through our own unique perspectives

Will there be nothing left to write about? Will I simply just close my notebook and sit back contemplating the next artistic challenge

All I know is that poetry fills that dark void inside of me, giving rise to a sense of calm that simply expels the sorrow from my soul

Mostly though, poetry fills me with the provocation to write more poetry, always querying that next combination of words to explain those impressions, just waiting for that passion for igniting the tip of my pen to fill those blank pages of my notebook with words of clarification

Yes, that's the problem with Poetry; it will never end; it will always gather the sorrow from my soul, pushing me to share those words for others to witness deep from inside of me

- Writer's Thoughts -

I realized one damp New England morning, as I walked along the Sea; I came across a fisherman drifting along in his boat. The scene reminded me of a painting by Andrew Wyeth. Its simplicity makes me think that the problem with poetry is it encourages the writing of more poetry. It made me realize this writing thing will never end; it will always solicit the sorrow from my soul, urging me to share my words for others to witness.

Art Credit - © Emma Eevantytär
@emma.eevantytar

"Lovers and madmen have such seething brains, such shaping fantasies, that apprehend more than cool reason ever comprehends.

The lunatic, the lover, and the poet are of imagination all compact: One sees more devils than vast hell can hold, that is, the madman: the lover, all as frantic, sees Helen's beauty in a brow of Egypt.

The poet's eye, in a fine frenzy, rolling, doth glance from heaven to earth, from earth to heaven; as imagination bodies forth, the forms of things unknown, the poet's pen turns them into shapes and gives to airy nothing, a local habitation, and a name."

—— Shakespeare William Shakespeare

JUST A POET

My unconstrained way of poetry allows me to express that individuality, digging into the profundities of my soul. With those abstract musings, I can confess those complex views of my professed realities

It may not be that ideal cup of poetic tea, but fortunately for me, the seeds of my passion for utterances were sown long ago by the Shakespeare's, Poe's, Cohen's, and Cumming's of the world

Yes, I'm just a poet of imagination expressing those devils from my hell's past, glancing from heaven to earth, from earth to heaven to write that poetry

Yes, I may not be someone's cup of poetic tea, but I am indeed just a poet, confessing those complex views of my professed realities

- Writer's Thoughts -

My soul dwelled in darkness, then along came poetry, a place that brought clarity to complex introspections.

Artist Credits - © Erin Murphy
@erin_murphy_art

"Let me, O let me bathe my soul in colors;
let me swallow the sunset and drink the rainbow."

—— Khalil Gibran

COLOR OF POETRY

Poetry has fondled my brain every letter written striving to entertain as my insights embark on a that literary journey

As that poem begins to unravel so do those lines of lyrical quandaries consuming my stories - evoking a canvas of colors from within my soul, those dark tones of words we call poetry

Putting that interjection at the end of those passages to compliment those verbs reflecting a mood - each revealing a little bit more of a personality

Those colors of poetic phrases never ceasing to amaze, that canvas of craft within my soul shaping the words of thoughts

Those hues fondling my brain with every letter written aspiring to entertain... those colors of my Poetry that I rely on to amuse

- Writer's Thoughts -

Those colors of poetry shaping our literary moods, for me those moments seem to be my most inspirational. With the colors of a rainbow projecting words of happiness, just as those hues of darkness dispatch the demons from my soul for all to witness.

Artist Credit - © Airesh Kate Caliso
@sketches_by_aika

"I have tried in my way to be free."

—— Leonard Cohen

IT WAS ME ALL ALONG

It was that time; when my life started somewhere in Europe that it all began
It was that time; when we moved to the Bayous that I began to be different
It was that time; as much as I tried, that reality revealed that I didn't fit in
It was that time; I became someone I wasn't supposed to be
It was that time; I left my home to serve my country as a naive young man
that I began to appreciate why I was so isolated from who I wanted to be

It was that time; I found myself roaming the paved streets of the big city, the dusty roads of the backcountry, the glacier fields of the north, the snow-covered mountains to the west, the tropical heat of Southeast Asia, the sandy deserts of the Middle East, those tropical islands of the Pacific Rim, and countless other austere places around the globe, that I eventually understood who I was

I discovered that it was me, the different one; it was me who didn't fit; it was me, the person I didn't want to be

All along, it was simply just me

- Writer's Thoughts -

All I wanted was to live a life where I could be me,
the person I didn't want to be.

Artist Credits - © Zen Artist Paul Quintero
@zen_art_time

Be still. Stillness reveals the secrets of eternity."
—— Lao Tzu

The artist Paul Quintero is a Zen monk and an accomplished artist. A Disciple of T. Deshimaru 1981. I first discovered Paul's artistic talents while searching for inspiration to write Zen Haiku Poetry. After seeing his wonderful Zen Sketches, I immediately recognized his gift for balancing art with the wisdom of Zen.

His inspiring words of Zen wisdom and art always provide me with a sense of peaceful repose, with an emptied stillness. This selected piece of art consoles me to rest in the present moment, finally feeling a composure that my words have been rummaging for, a repose of simplicity.

SILENCE

It's like I'm out here all alone with silence consuming me; in this moment of lull, my thoughts are their loudest, screaming; they exaggerate me to the fringe of obsession

The deafening silence besets me as much as I protest it; the darkest recesses overwhelm my thoughts entirely; my words become unclear; I focus on images; when images become distorted,
 I focus on the serenity of the pure silence

In this noiseless state, free of distraction, free of clamor and judgment, comfortable in this peaceful pause of my solitude

At last, it becomes clear in silence that my life has a peaceful stillness

-Writer's Thoughts -

I am at peace
Drifting like waves in the sea
Gliding like soft clouds in a quiet sky

With an emptied stillness
Rummaging for
Harmonious serenity
A balanced body and soul
With tranquility in equanimity
Seeking

Clarity through my observations
To rest in the present moment
With a repose of simplicity
I am finally at peace

DEAR BROTHER

Brother, I would love to say, "Hope all is well," that would be the appropriate words for an admired brother. However, given our history, it would be an ambiguous portrayal of my pure fervor and sentiments for your well-being

Understanding these words is intended to put closure to what we both have tolerated over the past fifty years. I hope you can understand the lack of empathy toward our problematic relationship

I don't know; maybe it's because of all the times you were so arrogant in your beliefs that the firstborn is far superior to their siblings

I don't know; maybe it's that time that you took a psychology class in college and felt it necessary to tinker with your younger brother's tender vulnerable mind with your psychological babble bull shit

I don't know; maybe it was that time you enabled your younger brother to alcohol and drugs before he was even aware of the dangers; oh, by the way, I still fight the afflictions of addiction

I don't know; maybe it was that time I joined the military and was home on furlough; instead of being proud of my achievement and success, you told me the military was a " parasite on society," hence calling me the same

I don't know; maybe at family holiday gatherings, your alcohol consumption and narcissistic personality always ended in our dear father, rest his soul, breaking up our arguments

For sure, it was that time I drove over 1000 miles to attend our father's funeral; when it came time for me to pay my final respects, you rushed the casket closed, urging the procession on to the cemetery before I had a chance to tell my father how much I loved and would miss him

I don't know, maybe the list of my hatred towards you is just too long to articulate in this brief letter, or perhaps it just doesn't matter at this point in our lives

Yes, maybe I shouldn't hold so much contempt for you in your old age; perhaps I should show some compassion for an aging narcissistic old man.

In the end, I know it does not matter, for I know you're a vile person who doesn't deserve my compassion or love

Regards, Your Younger Brother

- Writer's Thoughts -

This poem was written to put `Closure` for a lifetime of sibling rivalry, arrogance and egotism between two brothers. Sadly, that time of closure has come.

Artist Credits - © Eskander Dawani
@iskander.dawani

Artist Credit – © Pita Nketiah
@piteah

"The burdens in our minds are always heavier than the burdens on our shoulders!"

—— Mehmet Murat ildan

CARRYING BURDENS

Today, my soul feels like it's carrying a heavy burden, not knowing what anxieties will conflict inside of me, just listening to the horrors of my introspections

Today, my body feels plagued by old sadness that occasionally consumes me without provocation, hindering my sanity

Today, I reached an absurd conclusion, conceding to a sadness clambering from the depths of my soul, leaving me powerless and devoid of purpose and clarity

At the end of this day, all that remains is what remained yesterday and will remain tomorrow, just my soul carrying a heavy burden, searching for its sanity

- Writer's Thoughts -

Sometimes our burdens become so overwhelming that they're all we can think about, reaching the point where they feel like part of who we are. But we are not our burdens. Our burdens affect our confidence, weighing us down and not offering anything in return.

Artist Credit - © Airesh Kate Caliso
@sketches_by_aika

Once I could imagine my soul, I could imagine my death.
When I imagined my death, my soul died.
This I remember clearly.
My body persisted.
Not thrived but persisted
Why I do not know.
—— Louise Glück's

"Echoes."

A WILTING SOUL

I've tried to write this pain away to evict it from my head; it seems the more I try, the more my soul has decided it's goin' die

After everything that my tired soul has been through, after all this time, being lost in the dark, torn apart from its woes, it still strives to deprive that spirit of mine of the peace it deserves

There's no escaping it, despising it, wanting that feeling to go away, just so cold, just so dark, it seems like it's just my fate; there it stays, it won't leave me in peace, sucking life into a faded consummation

Enduring, not burgeoning, but persevered, my soul has become silent. That silence only speaks to those afflictions that propagate my anxieties

I've tried, believe me, I have tried, but it's all that past despair, the nothingness that numbs, grinds that soul that has perished inside of me

That soul of mine deciding it's just goin' to wilt away and die, and I don't know why

- Writer's thoughts -

My soul toils, weary from the anxieties of endeavoring to belong to this world.

Artist Credits - © Eskander Dawani
@iskander.dawani

I wrote "Set Me Free" in support of Domestic Violence Awareness Month. I hoped that by sharing my own story through these words of darkness, I could touch others to know they are not alone.

—— JNM

SET ME FREE

Raised in a world of untruths, through a life of misuse, victimized by the occurrences of constant abuse, suffering without impunity from those misrepresentations, torn, battered, and confused, only to be misled by the keepers of my youth

Cultivated in a life of false realities, shackled to a life of wrongful consequences, left alone with a voice never heard nor seen

Entombed by my own insecurities, waiting for an end that would set me free, knowing there was no escape from those horrors, alone and withdrawn with my inescapable consequences, just needing to be set free before it was too late - just needing to be set free

- Writer's Thoughts -

It was living in hell from one day to the next. Feeling like there was nothing I could do to flee. I didn't know where to go if I even tried. I feel powerless in my emotional dungeon to be set free before it's too late. - words from my younger self

Artist Credit – © Darya Karabchuk
@darya_karabchuk

"Every man has his secret sorrows which the world knows not, and often we call a man cold when he is only sad."

—— Henry Wadsworth Longfellow

MY DARK LABYRINTH

I often reminisce how as a young man, I wandered through the deep recesses of a dark mind searching for a life far away from this pain

Holding on to a spirit that had diminished from the torments of an afflicted soul, pondering those perturbations that weighed heavy on a young man's mind, those turmoils that deprived youthful ambitions

Treading gently into the labyrinth of my dark mind searching for atonement, looking for a path through contemplations, straying into those mad intensities, embracing the dark sorrow, exploring for a way to alchemize those past wounds

Longing for peace, a peace that seemed so far away, just scouring for a passage far away from that pain

-Writer's Thoughts -

The labyrinth is perhaps one of the oldest and most mysterious symbols known to mankind. It has been looked upon as an object of fear and hope. It has been perceived as a representation of hell and redemption. For me, that dark, mysterious symbol always gave me hope, discovering through this dark journey an acknowledgment, listening to its truth, and speaking it back to you through my poetry.

Artist Credit – © Darya Karabchuk
@darya_karabchuk

"A moment of serendipity is a wink from destiny."

—— Efrat Cybulkiewicz

SERENDIPITY

Grappling with those occurrences in life, wondering what defines our destination and what compels those ambitions to sprinkle life's complexities the way it does

What are those things so deep inside that they confuse - Why are we even driven to do the things we do

Chasing those inevitable outcomes, enduring toils along the way with all its chaos in between

The magic of uncertainty, it's that curiosity that dictates my lure, it's what serves that reverie deep inside that spirit of mine

It's life's unknown serendipitous discoveries not sought for but given anyway that steers me to the abstraction with all its improvisation

That unsuspecting raw world mining deep into my soul, appealing to the spontaneity of my words; It's just simply serendipity, it's just meant to be, those words residing deep inside of me

-Writer's Thoughts -

Serendipity: Such a beautiful word describing the occurrence of events by chance. I like to think it's the energy you put into the world, returning it with the magic of serendipitous discoveries.

Photography Credit – © Subhrodwip Karmakar
@subhrodwip_karmakar

"Each of us is born with a box of matches inside us

but we can't strike them all by ourselves"

—— Laura Esquivel

FIRE WITHIN

There's this fire deep inside of me; I have no idea where it came from or what it wants of me; maybe it's simply a rebirth of what already resides within me

That flame with all its colors strutting around into the darkness of the depths of my imagination

That flame is just lingering around, kindling my soul, craving those gentle embers, transporting me from that dark void with nothing but a glimmer of hope

That provocation, smoldering inside of me, setting a soul ablaze before it's too late before that flame burns out; It's just that fire that resides deep within me

- Writer's Thoughts -

Let your fire glimmer to those who want to know your light before that flame burns out before it's too late.

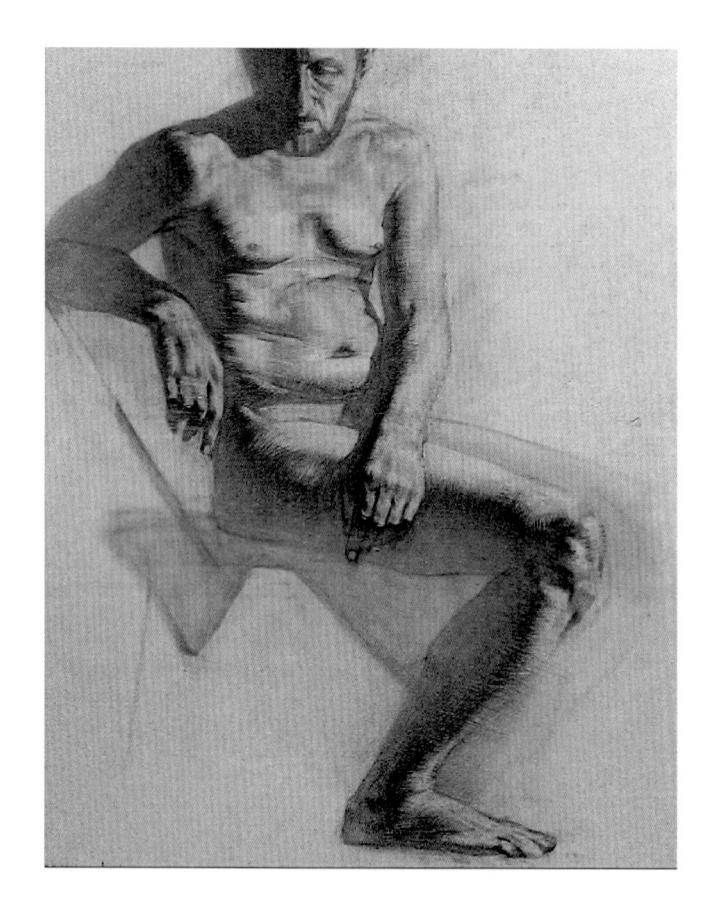

Artist Credit – © Darya Karabchuk
@darya_karabchuk

"You must suffer me to go my own dark way."

—— Robert Louis Stevenson,

DON'T WANNA BE A BURDEN ANYMORE

My soul's been a burden to me since I don't know when; these emotional chains that shackle my brain are of my own doing, soaking those tears of the past in the waters of my sanctity

Forever pushing the boundaries of life, finally paying the price for those improprieties, suffering in my dark realities, fearing that judgment, labeling my guilt as a burden to my insecurities

That burden from my past wants to just bury it with the shame that I carry around inside, something that needs to be finally put to rest before it devours me

That feeling of guilt, shame, the hurt of my pain, the decay of my brain feeds that hideous remorse

I just don't wanna carry that load anymore, don't wanna battle those demons anymore - just don't wanna be a burden anymore

- Writer's thoughts -

Battling so many things in our stride, we become entangled in chaos in this life journey. Like a lame creature, burdened and emotionally disquieted, I carry those burdens alone, feeling guilt, shame, and the hurt of my pain.

Artist Credit - © Airesh Kate Caliso
@sketches_by_aika

"One writes primarily to free oneself from oneself."

—— Marty Rubin

HE JUST WROTE

He wrote out his rage with perplexity, slowly coming to terms with his truths and realities

He wrote with an intention to unload memories, writing with strong acuity, releasing that hostility, that sadness through the repetition of his words

He wrote to allow others to peer into his soul, to feel his pain, to feel that connection of emotions from deep inside

He wrote to tell a story, a testimony, to give witness to; he just wrote off the truths from within, disclosing a resentment, releasing with a fury that controversy through the repetition of his words

He just wrote

- Writer's Thoughts -

I've realized the good thing about writing is the catharsis I feel when everything finally comes out. It's as though I've written with tears of bitterness, releasing a fury that didn't have to be inside me anymore.

Artist Credits – © Yeimei Wangsa
@ymei_iem

"It is a great art to have an abundance of knowledge and experience - to know the richness of life, the beauty of existence, the struggles, the miseries, the laughter, the tears - and yet keep your mind very simple; and you can have a simple mind only when you know how to love."

—— Jiddu Krishnamurti

SIMPLICITY

I used to think I was a complex thinker - understanding those complicated hypotheses, reading those books of philosophies, solving those intricate speculations of theory

I used to think - complicating matters made me feel good about myself as if overcoming some immense intricacies, jumping from one thing to the next without a second introspection

I used to think - I was an unyielding type of fellow, always with a focused smile, living life intoxicated through my difficulties

Lately, I've been thinking about peeling back some of those complicated layers, sensing more to me than meets the eye; maybe, it's something called simplicity

- Writer's Thoughts -

In this busy world, sometimes simplicity can be hard to find. Everything is alive, frantic, and harried; people jump from one thing to the next without a second thought.

Finding the time to slow down, appreciate the simple things, and embrace the calm, the simple, and the peaceful parts of the world is a rare joy, but it's one that some people enjoy every day.

Artist Credits - © Eskander Dawani
@iskander.dawani

"The loneliest moment in someone's life is when they are watching their whole world fall apart, and all they can do is stare blankly."

—— F. Scott Fitzgerald

LONELY MEMORIES

Maybe If –

we just hadn't run out of words to say; maybe if we had just spoken up, or maybe if we weren't so afraid to speak our truths

Maybe If –

we just had tossed a stone into the sea, wishing for that hurt to go away; instead of craving for our souls to be saved or striving for our broken hearts to mend, we could have wished for those guilty recalls to fade

Maybe If –

our desires had never dried up; our appetites never waned, leaving that pain that never healed

Maybe, just maybe –

if we hadn't allowed ourselves to weaken, knowing that a flame still kindled within, maybe those desires would've never smoldered into ashes of our memories

Maybe, just maybe - we wouldn't be so lonely

- Writer's Thoughts -

Just reflections from a life from long ago.

Artist Credits – © Darya Karabchuk
@darya_karabchuk

"He's like a hero come back from the war, a poor maimed bastard living out the reality of his dreams.

Wherever he sits, the chair collapses; whatever door he enters the room is empty: Whatever he puts in his mouth leaves a bad taste. Everything is just the same as it was before; The elements are unchanged; team is no different than the reality.

Only, between the time he went to sleep and the time he woke up, his body was stolen."

— Henry Miller

A SOLDIER'S DREAMS

Those dreams that once lived within me were always a symbol of hope

Those dreams with a simplicity of proportion, with an innocence that provoked me into a better way

Those dreams are always there for me with a great sense of serenity, bringing courage to persevere, a solitude of truce

Those dreams were shattered by the servitude of service, leaving only a hint of the possibilities of pleasure once again

Those damn dreams that once promised a better way are now broken and stolen from a memory of a time; it's just the same as before

- Writer's Thoughts -

Soldiers always dream of better days; as a young man, I had many such dreams during service to my country. The afflictions of my servitude eventually eroded them. Those dreams that once promised a better way are no more.

Artists Credit – © Subhrodwip Karmakar
@subhrodwip_karmakar

"My imagination functions much better when I don't have to speak to people."

—— Patricia Highsmith

SOLITUDE

Why do I feel the need to be alone to ponder those uncertainties of contrition with my solitude

Why is it? I prefer the seclusion of a peaceful paradise without companions who would only serve to confuse my acuities in this comforting isolation

Why is it easier to be without conversation, just preferring face-to-face time with my thoughts, appreciating the sounds of my soul for its simple complicity

Why is it that those words of simplicity always offer me so much harmony, reassuring while soothing those uncertainties of contrition in my solitude

- Writer's Thoughts -

Solitude is my creative place, offering consoling impressions of inspiration by being alone. Solitude is a gift that only a few people understand.

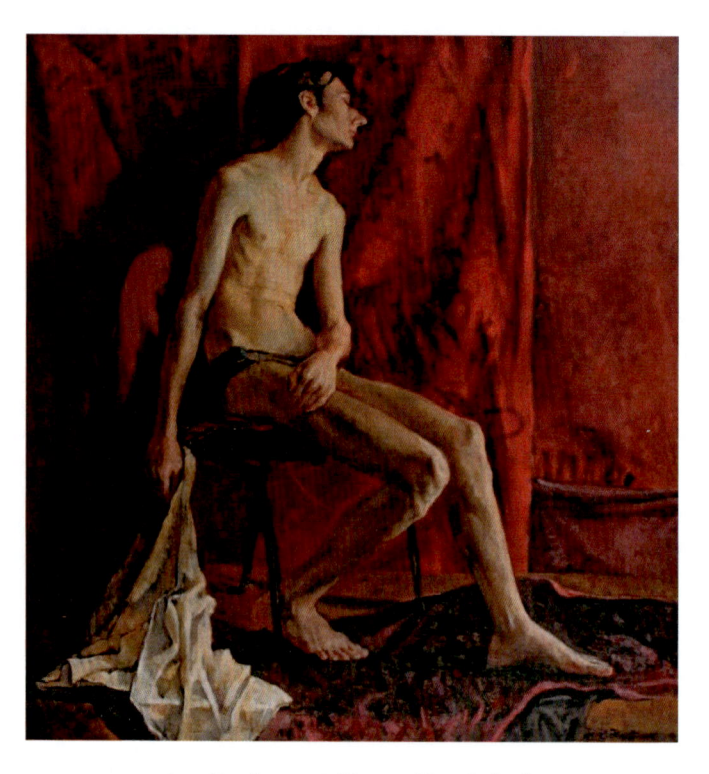

Art Credits – © Darya Karabchuk
@darya_karabchuk

"If you say we are the same.
Why do you then want to be treated differently and special?
If you say you are different.
Why do you want to change me to be like you?"

—— De philosopher DJ Kyos

WHOM I'M SUPPOSED TO BE

In this darkness, I often wonder if I am already precisely who I'm supposed to be

I stay here in this dark place out of fear, that fear of judgment, that fear of scorn, most of all, that fear of abandonment

I'm afraid that if I depart this dark solitary safe space, what possibly waits beyond might be a much greater uncertainty

Or it might be an opportunity, to be exactly whom I'm supposed to be

- Writer's Thoughts -

I wrote this piece in support of the LGBTQ community during Pride Month.

From music and fashion to political action, there are a million ways to express your LGBTQ Pride; I have chosen to express my support through the arts and poetry. This poem was inspired by a piece of art by Darya Karabchuk, one of my favorite contemporary artists.

Artist Credit – © Subhrodwip Karmakar
@subhrodwip_karmakar

"As I grow older, much older, I will experience many things, and I will hit rock bottom again and again. Again and again, I will suffer; again, and again I will get back on my feet. I will not be defeated. I won't let my spirit be destroyed."

—— Banana Yoshimoto

STOLEN SPIRIT

This abuse of mine seems always to be out there controlling my mind, with darkness preying on my emotional confidence, devouring my prosperity

Just when I think I'm free from the cruelty, it cultivates itself again, feeding on my contentment, cueing itself through mental suggestion that I'm nothing without those insults, nothing without that humiliation, nothing without that manipulation of my happiness, that I am nothing without that misuse

Damn...those gaslighting influences, I'm here just tryin' to remember that autonomy that I once enjoyed - somehow hiding those delicate scars revealing a serenity that doesn't reside within me anymore - realizing so little from a peace that never came - conceding a stolen spirit from so long, long ago

- Writer's Thoughts -

The only person that deserves a special place in your life is someone that never made you feel like you were an option in theirs.

Artist Credit – © Subhrodwip Karmakar
@subhrodwip_karmakar

"What is in question as I stand
Safely at the border of myself
And think of leaping
Or continuing on?

What happens when I walk
To the extent of "I"
And then keep walking?
Who am I then?"

—— Eric Overby

WHO I WAS

I have this feeling I've been there before; I can see myself becoming who I want to be, looking through that perspective, knowing after tomorrow, I'll see a different me, maybe like the one I used to be

Wondering if I paused time, could I remember exactly what it felt like to be me - like who I was before

Wondering If I take that next step back to who I was, will I respect it before it all goes away

Wondering, if I don't look beyond - can I remember who I was before - before it's all gone

- Writer's Thoughts -

Like a picture out of focus, I'm starting to think I don't even know who I am anymore. I'm not who I think I am; I only experience life through whom I want to be.

Artist Credits - © Airesh Kate Caliso
@sketches_by_aika

"Memories saturate my heart,
and the story of you spills from my eyes."

— Grace Andren

BORN STILL

A child spent an entire life at birth, not allowed entrance to this world, but carried to death before life could even begin

Not given even one glimpse into a world it would never know, not even one word spoken, just a deep silence as passing devoured a fragile soul

Not even a cry from initiating life, only lonely desperation, flying unaided into darkness, endeavoring to hold on, weakening to change a fate, darkness of what would never be

Along the way, something did change when that spirit departed; a soul became hardened, resolved, like a piece of raw steel fractured at its core

Losing that tender spirit back into the heavens, just wishing it would have been given that one chance to fly as an angelic sparrow on its own

That child that was born still to the darkness of what would never be

- Writer's Thoughts -

When a child dies before birth, you never get to hear that first voice nor witness life from their eyes. Still, that child lived; it came into this world. That existence was real.

In these words, I seek consolation with my memories of a soul born still that was never given a chance to fly like a sparrow.

Artist Credit - © Sara Fatah Samsom
@sroo_as16

"If you hear a voice within you say you cannot paint, then by all means paint and that voice will be silenced."

— Vincent Willem Van Gogh

DOUBT

Damn that self-doubt of uncertainties, why does it always creep up on me, competing for my sanity

Always thinkin' about those anxieties, spotlighting my misgivings, serving as an affliction without hesitation

Bringing with it those scars of sensitivities, never without warning, playing tricks on my mind, exposing weak vulnerabilities by sharing those insecurities

Shaming me, causing doubt within me, becoming my own worst enemy, that damn self-doubt inside of me

- Writer's Thoughts -

I seek strength, not to be greater than others, but to fight my greatest enemy, the doubts within myself. That's why I write these words of poetry.

Artist Credits - © Eskander Dawani
@iskander.dawani

"Supposedly she'd died, but here she was again–somewhat changed, but you couldn't kill her. Not when the truest part of her hadn't even been born."

—— Denis Johnson,

ALREADY DEAD

There's a demon who askin' for me by name, sayin' it's time to extinguish that flame

I was telling him the other day, you might put me to rest, but you're never goin' to take away my pain

I told him when he comes to harvest my soul, don't matter cause, the future ahead is already dead

I've been hearing that beast knocking at my door, I've told him once, I told him twice he's already been here before, I explained, it was the wrong time, I told him to take the blame, cause' it was not my time to relinquish that flame

But now, I know what the future ahead bestows, you can put me to rest, but you're never goin' to take away that pain, cause that beast has already staked claim to my soul, you see, I'm already dead

- Writer's Thoughts -

To live in the moment is vastly different from living for it. To be truly present as life unfolds around one is to take the fullest advantage of being alive. I have seen death many times, somehow, always negotiating for another day. I feel the reaper has already made his case, he can put me to rest but never going to take away my pain, cause, I'm already dead.

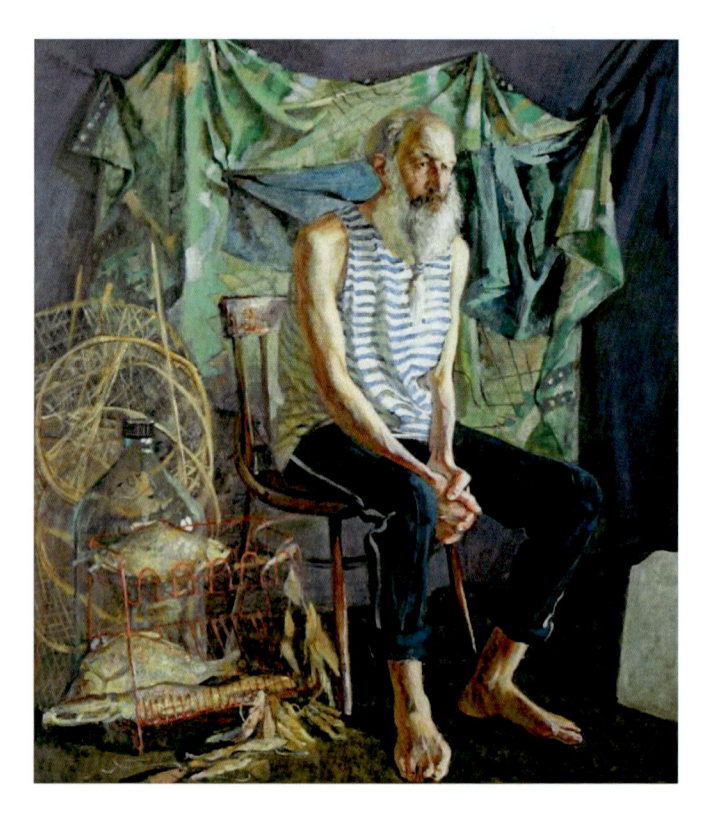

Art Credits – © Darya Karabchuk
@darya_karabchuk

I find solace in my diary, losing myself in those scribbled recollections. Sometimes though, it scares the hell out of me the way my soul becomes so numb when all those pages turn into blank canvases waiting to be darkened with new possibilities.

—— Thoughts from the Author

MY DIARY

I sit alone with my reflections feeling like I got a lot of meditations, jus' needing to write that sadness away, looking for my diary to file those contemplations away

Anxious, not knowing what to do, 'cause there's no one else to turn to, I can't talk it away, so I tell it to my diary, too many questions, too many scrutinizes, not enough explanations

I sit alone with my deliberations thinkin' ain't no use in struggling, wondering if I'm the one in need of psychotherapy, every day just seems more difficult to cope, I feel like I'm the one holding on to that proverbial lifeline of hope

Can't seem to keep my mind on a steady path, just living vicariously through an unsettled past, writin' it away in that diary for my sanity

- Writer's Thoughts -

This piece is based loosely on the influence from my readings of the Diary of a Madman: The Geto Boys, Life, Death, and the Roots of Southern Rap of Brad "Scarface" Jordan

Artist Credits - © Indi Henri
@the_apologetic_

"We choose our joys and sorrows long before we experience them."

—— Khalil Gibran

FAREWELL

I want to know when I can say farewell to this sadness that travels alongside this existence of mine

Thinkin' I should give myself some time to figure out what this agonizing is all about, wrestling with those brief winks of solitude I've known from time to time

Looking for a place to ease that pain, searching through those silent contemplations pursuing a calm that I've locked away in a place called sanity

Aware that by the end of this day, all that will remain is what remained yesterday and will remain tomorrow, just a spirit carrying with it a quiet introspection desiring a peace that may never come its way

Just wantin' to finally bid adieu to the hold that this burden has on my soul

- Writer's Thoughts -

When I think about my pain, I often wonder if it will ever fade. Understanding, I'm the only one that can decide how long I will let it torment me. Some days though, the unsatisfying mornings tells me I am your future; here is your baggage of sorrow; I'm here to stay.

THOSE LOVE THINGS

"We are not mad. We are human.
We want to love,
And someone must forgive us for the paths we take to love,
For the paths are many and dark,
And we are ardent and cruel in our journey."

—— Leonard Cohen

"My reputation as a ladies' man was a joke that caused me to laugh bitterly through the ten thousand nights I spent alone."
—— Leonard Cohen

Artist Credits - © Pita Nketiah
@piteah

"A pen went scribbling along.
When it tried to write love, it broke."

—— Rumi

THOSE LOVE THINGS

I want to write that poetry about love things, seems like each time I try; I get stuck within my broken soul

I expect to find those perfect words of passion, only to be led astray through my vulnerabilities

Wanting to write those words deep from within that's starved to be devoured by expressions of love, only to scribble those things that leave me lonesome with a cheated heart

Here I am, just tryin' to write that poetry about those love things, but yet once again, I'm penning those dark thoughts that reside deep within me

- Writer's Thoughts -

If I could just write when I'm at peace, thinking it wouldn't have the same gloomy outcome. All I want to do is write poetry about those love things.

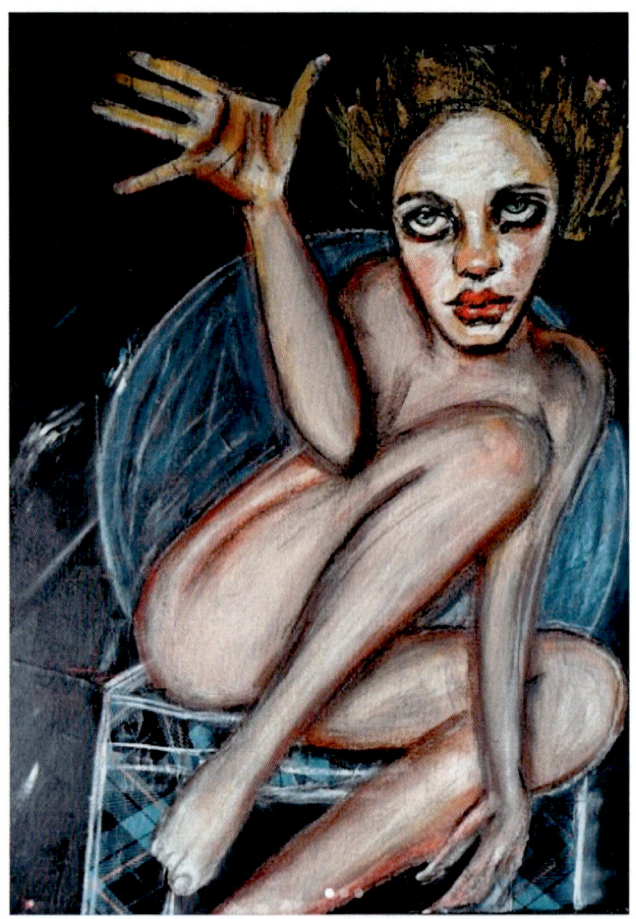

Artist Credits - © Pita Nketiah
@piteah

"The most terrible poverty is loneliness and the feeling of being unloved."

—— Mother Teresa

ABANDONED AND LONELY

I didn't think you would abandon me; I ought to have known better, don't know why I'd speculate you wouldn't leave me when I was down and out; I couldn't even ponder that as a possibility

Even when you were wrong, I always wanted you to be right, even though I knew it to be untrue; if only you'd seen the good in me, even when those times were agonizing, I was always tryin' to hold you tight

Even when you were lost and alone and couldn't find your way back home - I found you and brought you to where you were supposed to be, next to me

Even when you were hurtin' from all that pain, I was there to wipe those tears away, knowing you'd be just fine, 'cause I never left your side, even when you were down and out

I just didn't think you'd leave me abandoned and lonely; I ought to have known better; I couldn't, I wouldn't even have pondered that as a possibility

- Writer's Thoughts -

I'm a hopeless romantic who seems to fall in love with ease. I always thought it just meant that I could see the beauty in most of the people who cross paths with me, appreciating it for what it is and what it isn't. Love can be imperfect. Falling for someone's flaws is just as necessary as falling for their strengths.

Artist Credits - © Eskander Dawani
@iskander.dawani

"I was falling through time and space and stars and sky and everything in between. I fell for days and weeks and what felt like a lifetime across lifetimes. I fell until I forgot I was falling."

—— Jess Rothenberg

FALLING

I don't know how it always happens; somehow, I manage to fall for those beautiful souls - it's like I got no control over it

You'd have thought that I had better sense, thinking by now, I would simply just know better - speculating as much as I try, I'm powerless to control those urges of mine, placing me in those junctures of unbridled complications

I just can't help myself from being devoured by my good intentions; I can't seem to constrain those desires, always falling for those captivating souls

You'd think by now, I would simply just know better, you know, falling for those enchanting souls

- Writer's Thoughts -

People who know me know that I fall in love easily. It just means I can see the beauty in most people who cross paths with me. I appreciate it for what it is and for what it isn't.

Love is imperfect. Falling for someone's flaws is just as necessary as falling for their strengths. And people like me, who fall into love easily, are sometimes the loneliest souls around at the end of the day.

Artist Credits - © Eskander Dawani
@iskander.dawani

"He'll never be able to hide his feelings for you when he sees you. That's the thing with enduring love. It can stay buried, you can deny it, but once you are near that person, those feelings pull you together like a magnetic bond."

—— Jacqueline Simon Gunn

EVEN WHEN I SHOULDN'T BE

I think about you, even when I shouldn't be
I feel that enduring love for you, thinking someone may have written a poem or two about this love thing that lingers deep inside me

These verses composed over and over in my head
Those rhyming words about how my heart can't fail you
How my thoughts recall a gentle warm touch, how my eyes stole glances of a tender smile that now seems so far, far away

Sometimes, I feel like I must have loved you too much because these days, I find myself writing this poetry by myself in lonesome solitude

Writing these reflections of love about the rarest of flowers that used to caress my soul, now just becoming distant memories, as I think about you even when I shouldn't be

As this love thing lingers deep inside of me

- Writer's Thoughts -

In my solitude, pondering those love things, I always remember the way it felt deep down in my soul.

Recalling that when love is enduring, even when it becomes just a distant memory, you think about it even when you shouldn't be.

Artist Credits - © Erin Murphy
@erin_murphy_art

"The room was large and empty except for a four-poster bed and a framed picture of Marie Laveau, the voodoo queen of New Orleans. A free woman of color who owned her own business, she made her own name and rose to fame and power in a segregated South."

—— Margot Berwin,

"Scent of Darkness"

STARLIGHT ON THE BAYOU

Those goosebumps first tugged my scrutiny; she had this rawness about her, seemingly always desperately painful in her naked expression; there was never a warmth with her, always that sunless shadow of darkness that followed

Those eyes could possess and steal your soul if you allowed them to

In the back room, she had shelves filled with mason jars meant for those voodoo spells, bizarre concoctions intended to heal, inflict illness, and discard memories with countless other purposes

Speaking in tongues calling my name, bringing in the twilight, she summoned me to bleed one more time, to let the moon guide her witchery, to let the spirits be right, possessing and stealing my soul

Sometimes I still feel those goosebumps, not recalling that much with my discarded memories and all

Surely, stored on her shelves filled with mason jars meant for those voodoo spells, when she possessed and stole my soul

- Writer's Thoughts -

Voodoo is very old black magic - possibly one of the oldest forms of all time. From my neck of the woods, it's often referred to as vodou or voudoun .

Voodoo worships the loa, which are literally spirits like ghosts - but much more powerful. The Voodoo priestess can summon the loa, and the spirit inhabits her body.

Artist Credits - © Eskander Dawani
@iskander.dawani

"A painful thorn on a black rose,
With such elegance, she bears it all."

—— Unknown

MY BLACK ROSE

She was like a provocative Black Rose, alluring but elusively rare, blooming in front of our eyes - desired by all, cultivated by none

Those raw eyebrows eased down gently to her black chic eyelashes. An artist could not have painted her any sweeter

Her beguiling, pearly white teeth lit up the room when she broke into a smile. Filed to perfection, her crimson red fingernails ran through her dark black hair. Spools of it plunged around her silhouette-perfect face, concealing a swan's neck, elegant and smooth

Her nebulous, devouring eyes sparkled with the 'joie de vivre'
 they were like two embers penetrating the darkness

Her lush lips whispered in a lyrical voice as sweet as any songbird. Her voguish clothes kept captive an aroma redolent of cinnamon and meadow-fresh mint. It lingered in the room long after she had gone

That remarkable Black Rose, elusive and provocatively rare, blooming in front of our eyes - Desired by all, cultivated by none

- Writer's Thoughts -

I wrote this piece with thoughts back to a day when I left my home as a young man with the final advice given by a mother's loving console. That day, as I boarded a Greyhound bus to face my life's destiny, she calmly told me to watch out for those painted ladies that would be encountered along my journey.

Artist Credits - © Pita Nketiah
@piteah

"a flower knows when its butterfly will return, and if the moon walks out, the sky will understand; but now it hurts to watch you leave so soon when I don't know if you will ever come back."

—— Sanober Khan

ADIEU

On this day, my words of poetry seem to be fading into darkness, wanting to write words of passion, only to disclose those words of frailty, this ink of mine withering from nothingness that loiters for a truce deep inside my fragile soul

Usually, writing poetry that begins with those words of love for you, always culminating with the same poetic intention of unconditional love, but on this day, somewhere lost in the middle, there is a wounded spirit composing these words that I usually write to you

On this last day, these words of poetry struggle more than all those other days; because I still do love you more today than I did all those other yesterdays; I truly do

But on this lonely day, I bid you adieu, writing these last words of love poetry to you

- Writer's Thoughts -

Love is proved when you let go of someone because they need you to.

Artist Credits – © Rita Taha
@ritta.taha

"Beware when you fall in love with an artist, be it a painter, a singer, or a poet, for the artist will paint you with strokes and hues in shapes of every kind, sing about you with heartbreak lyrics and feelings that rhyme, write about you with the simplest words and a secret message they want to say beware of the artist and their love one wrong move, and you're an artwork in their display."

—— Lunar

WRITIN' THAT PROSE

To write that love prose just for you, there's one thing I must do; it's to cultivate this poetry about that love thing with thoughts of you

Unfailingly starting with that seductive smile, such a lovely place to begin, reminding me how it felt when a soul was first captured via my heart

Those words of mine penned as couriers of art taking me to your alluring eyes, the softness of your skin, and the shape of your delicious lips

With an insatiable desire, my quill composes verses of your curves, tracing along your slender carcass, describing the taste that only your warm sweetness can provide; these words of mine adoring everything about you, from your silky hair down to those manicured toes

It's that elegance, that beautiful way about you; it's that tender touch, every kiss, the softness of your soul, your supportive compassion, it's that commitment to our love

It's all these things I would write; it's those love things caressing my thoughts when I write this poetic prose just for you

- Writer's Thoughts -

Michelangelo, paint my poetry to perfection; Picasso turn the greatness of my words into a poetry of my love, for if true love were art, my soul would be the perfect prose written just for you.

Artist Credits –© Eskander Dawani
@iskander.dawani

"Never fall in love with stargazers – always with accelerated affection. Their love disappears in the blink of an eye like a shooting star."

—— RSCruz

FADING

I ask myself these days about those thoughts of poetry; how many times must I say, without hesitation, how many times must my soul write those words of adoration? It's always the same; telling myself just one more time; writing those words of poetry, just one more time for you

As I think about how you consoled my heart, whispered into that fragile soul of mine, and called upon a sense of longing in this weary old heart, sowing the seeds of passion for a love that had the possibility to bloom once again

Even now, as I endure your silence, as your spirit fades away from me, I still search for those perfect words of poetry. Even on the loneliest of nights without you, I still think about just writing those love things that I can't help but write just for you

Thinkin' about this devotion of mine that's truly absolute, even in your silent scarcity, still finding a way to write those words of prose to a fading love just for you

Telling myself just one more time, just one more time

- Writer's Thoughts -

In your life, you will meet shooting stars. You will see them, make your wish, and see them disappear.

Artist Credit - © Eskander Dawani
@iskander.dawani

"There is the heat of Love, the pulsing rush of Longing, the lover's whisper, irresistible—magic to make the sanest man go mad."

—— Homer, The Iliad

LONGING

Missing your voice, remembering how your inspiring way echoed into my heart, seemingly so close, yet so far away, so gentle, but now just whispering in silence

Still hearing the sweet comfort of your stillness, waiting in quiet solitude for your presence, with reflections of what was, now, just withering into the recesses of a meandering mind

With thoughts atilt, a heart that beats with the memory of a tenderness that longs for a time that was consumed by our passions, a time that once kindled our fascinations

Leaving a nothing, nothing but a lingering sense of solitude, for a resonance that once was

Those thoughts are purging the poetry from my soul; those thoughts from a spirit standing mute with the agony of longing for you

- Writer's Thoughts -

I wonder how much of the day is spent longing for things we desire that could have been, now just whispering in silent reflection.

Artist Credit - © Eskander Dawani
@iskander.dawani

"I love my friends
neither with my heart nor with my mind.
Just in case...
Heart might stop.
The mind can forget.
I love them with my soul.
Soul never stops or forgets."

—— Rumi

LEAN ON ME

I've found in you a bond that forever has transformed my life, you and me becoming one in a way that I knew would eternalize a change deep inside me

It's that affinity between us, offering me prospects of hope, making me think of being whole again; all I'm asking in exchange is to give these lonesome intentions a chance

Accepting you unconditionally, with all those faults and complexities offering you all my perspicuity of consent for you to lean on in those times of chaos

In your kindred nurtured devotion, I've found a spirit within, found those truths of my meaning, an unconditional tenderness that I, too, can lean on in times of dark adversity

Trusting that bond, transforming our lives forever; it's just you and me, it's what we do, offering our wisdom of consent to lean on in those times of complexities

- Writer's Thoughts -

I recently read a Rumi quote that influenced these thoughts of friendship. Reflecting on how unconditional tenderness can provide the prospects of hope just by providing an understanding of a sympathetic shoulder to lean on during times of dark adversity.

Artist Credits- © Pita Nketiah
@piteah

"Your heart and my heart are very, very old friends."

—— Rumi

EMBRACE

Sometimes - I daydream about running my fingers through your silky follicles, holding you in my arms, embracing your warmth next to my requesting soul, nourishing a gentle kiss on your tempting lips

Sometimes - I search for those deep moments of ardor with virtuous intentions, with a heart that aches with loneliness, provoking a softness that caresses my broken spirit

Sometimes - It's just the need that I wish for, that need I covet, those thoughts of devotion, wondering if this is how true love is meant to be

Sometimes - it's just those tender reflections of mine that capture a soul as it daydreams, returning to you each day, reminding me to love you more today than I have all of those other yesterdays

- Writer's Thoughts -

Sometimes the simple expression of the warmth of a hug from a love that has endured reminds us that true love grows with each passing day, getting stronger than it was on all those other yesterdays.

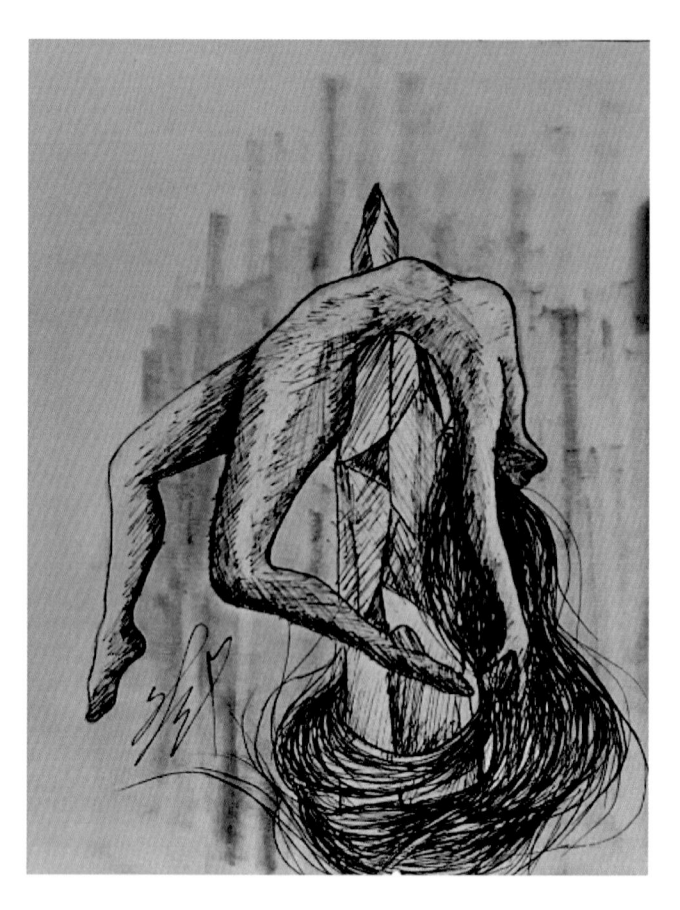

Artist Credits - © Sara Fatah Samsom
@sroo_as16

"Until you realize how easy it is for your mind to be manipulated, you remain the puppet of someone else's game."

—— Evita Ochel

ALL USED UP

Just been feeling all used up lately; no other way to put it; life is starting to feel like an old, tired addictive rerun

I was just fine being left in my own hallowed refuge; I wasn't anticipating having my vulnerabilities preyed upon by misguided intentions; it didn't take long for those thoughts of misuse to start sinking in

Been feeling like a casualty of manipulation, a device of twisted emotional gratification, like a puppet to someone else's a pastime

Routinely subjected to those subtle mind tricks, with a vicious need for a slanted control

Foraging on those euphoric feelings of mine, then threatening to take them away, like a drug dealer playing that dangerous game of addiction, enticing those weak vulnerabilities, manipulating with tricks of those mind control, making life feel like an old, tiring addictive rerun

Just been feeling all used up lately; no other way to put it

- Writer's Thoughts -

This featured piece of art, `A Pierced Soul,` initially fascinated me. My impression was of a woman all used up by the manipulate desires of a lover; becoming casualty of manipulation, a device of twisted emotional gratification, like a puppet to someone else's a pastime.

Artist Credits - © Erin Murphy
@erin_murphy_art

Erin Murphy's Art has always captivated me, with many inspiring impressions that constantly absorb and dominate my thoughts. This piece grabbed my attention. It reminds me that the unfortunate thing about love is that sometimes it does have an expiration date, sadly being replaced even after all the efforts to hold on.

—— JNM

WRITIN' FOR YOU

You got me writin' poetry just for you, even tho' the story is not new, you got me writin' the only poem I ever knew...

You got me writin' them words; ever since my eyes saw you, you got me thinkin' about writin' that poetry just for you

Even tho' your intentions are gone; I'm still thinkin' I need to carry on

Cause you got me writin' them verses, even tho' I'm so sad; you got me yearning for that passion we once had

You got me writin' that poetry just for you, even tho' I know it's untrue, those words I'm writin' just for you

Now I'm just old, thinkin' about all those words I used to write just for you

- Writer's Thoughts -

The unfortunate thing about being love's doormat is that eventually, you will expire and get replaced.

Artist Credits - © Pita Nketiah
@piteah

"Here's another poem, like all others before and after,
dedicated to you.
There isn't anything left to be said but I will spend my life trying to
put you into words.
You who is every goodness, every optimism and hope.
Your love is a better fate for me than anything I could wish for.
If you are a part of me, then you're the best part.
And if you're separate from me, then you are my destination.
But I've become a weary traveler, so please, let us never be apart."

—— Kamand Kojouri

LAST DANCE

As I sit with my thoughts, my mind is playing tricks on me, wondering if she was nothing but the scent of an old dream, just a distant memory fading from all the pictures that I remember, a recollection coming back only after a few glasses of whisky

In her letters written to me, those words were at the tip of my recall, knowing them all by heart, able to paint them from thin air onto that four-cornered canvas stuck on my wall

Wanting to remember those inconsistencies of our love stretching far past plausible borders

I should have seen it coming. Looking at her was dangerous; it was pain from the start; I never really enjoyed the part cause' it wasn't pretty, it wasn't smart; what happened to my heart when that love tumbled into the dark, as my mind began to play tricks on me

- Writer's Thoughts -

People think a soul mate is your perfect fit, and that's what everyone wants to believe. But a true soul mate's purpose is to shake you up, tear apart your ego a little bit, show you your obstacles and addictions, break your heart open so new light can get in, and make you so desperate and out of control that you must transform your life. But sometimes it's not always pretty; it's not always smart what can happen to the heart when love tumbles into the dark.

Artist Credits – © Vicki Sullivan
@0ne_flow

This piece of art devoured me the very instant I came across it. So many sensations consuming my thoughts, grabbing my attention, but it was "Those Bewitching Eyes" that seized my creativity... Compelling me to express my words to this enchanting piece of art...

—— JNM

BEWITCHING EYES

Those eyes intrigue, looking past what you can see, windows directly into the soul, without lies, revealing those truths

Those eyes reflected confidence, feeling secure and extensively sure of self-dignity, saying more than words ever could say

Those eyes unconscious but still a ravenous interpreters, only speaking to the language of our tears

Those uncomfortable eyes strewing over us like torches into the darkness, devouring our spirits

Those eyes reflect a past, present, and future with all the same outcome, pervading that dark sadness within

Those bewitching eyes, looking past what can be seen, windows into the soul without lies, telling those truths of our deepest remorseful regrets

Those Bewitching Eyes

- Writer's Thoughts -

The tongue may hide the truth but the eyes—will never lie, sometimes if you look deep enough, they will reflect a past, present, and future with all the same outcomes.

Artist Credits - © Debora Lapa
@artz_heartz_

"I'm always wondering about the what ifs,
about the road not taken."

—— Jenny Han

WHAT IF

What if in our absurdity, I lost you, in our absence to console each other, not being there when it was needed the most, renouncing what we had, searching, wandering, looking for a love that had strayed

What if we hadn't misplaced each other in that uninhibited emotional storm? Would our souls still be interlaced, or would they be devoid of that precious feeling we so covet

What if we had chosen a different path, you and me? Would we still suffer the same? Would it have eased our pain when you stole all the words to our story and drained my soul as you went away

What if; what if

- Writer's Thoughts -

What if, at times of crossroads, we simply just chartered different paths; What if all our pondering thoughts were just an absurdity anyway; would the words to our story still be the same?

Artist Credit - © Pita Nketiah
@piteah

"You can't be everybody's cup of tea, some like it bitter, some like it sweet Nobody's everybody's favorite, so you might as well just make it how you please You can't be, everybody's cup of tea, why would you want to be? "

—— Kacey Musgraves

MY CUP OF TEA

She is my cup of tea
With her, my life could be a jubilee
Wearing my best clothes and all
Making time, to place that call

But, don't you see
That girl is perfect for me
I've been waiting a whole life
For something just like this
Cause, she is my cup of tea

I just want her, to be all for me
That love would be a mystery
I hope she makes room for me
Cause, she is a once-in-a-lifetime cup of tea
But why would she want to be?

- Writer's Thoughts -

This piece of poetry is dedicated to that special someone in my life who may not be perfect. But she makes my life a Jubilee. She is my once-in-a-lifetime cup of tea.

Artist Credits - © Eskander Dawani
@iskander.dawani

"You looked at her like you looked at the moonlight through those windows. You looked at her like you'd just found another reason to believe in God."

—— Tiffany Reisz

MOONLIGHT SERENADE

You have touched my mind every bit of you seeming to amble,
Like the sweet music of a moonlight serenade
Each smile appears to hypnotize me as my intentions begin to travel,
As your beauty begins to unravel
Like lines of poetry making up devouring words
Arousing a canvas of art within my soul,
Your lustrous hue of this poetry I write for you
My love, for I belong to you
On this moonlight serenade

- Writer's Thoughts -

The Moonlight incites dark passions like a cold flame, making hearts burn with desire like a lover's serenade.

Artist Credits - © Eskander Dawani
@iskander.dawani

"It's very romantic to think of oneself as a lost soul, drifting like a cloud through life."

—— Marty Rubin

A LOST SOUL

Lost my way
Forgot to call
A cold heart beats
Tears lost in uncertainty
You are not here
You were always here

Now time forgets
As a heart rages on for directions
Your name only distorts my way
Everything seems like a vacant place
Waiting in my lost soul

I lost my way
I forgot to call
Now just a broken heart
Just a lost soul with shattered dreams
Who lost his way, now just full of pain

- Writer's Thoughts -

"A famous author once said that you couldn't go home again. But when you find you are lost, home is the only place to go. Remember the way, the stars will guide you. Your heart is her memory & the soul is your compass. And one day you will find her again."

—— R.M. Engelhardt

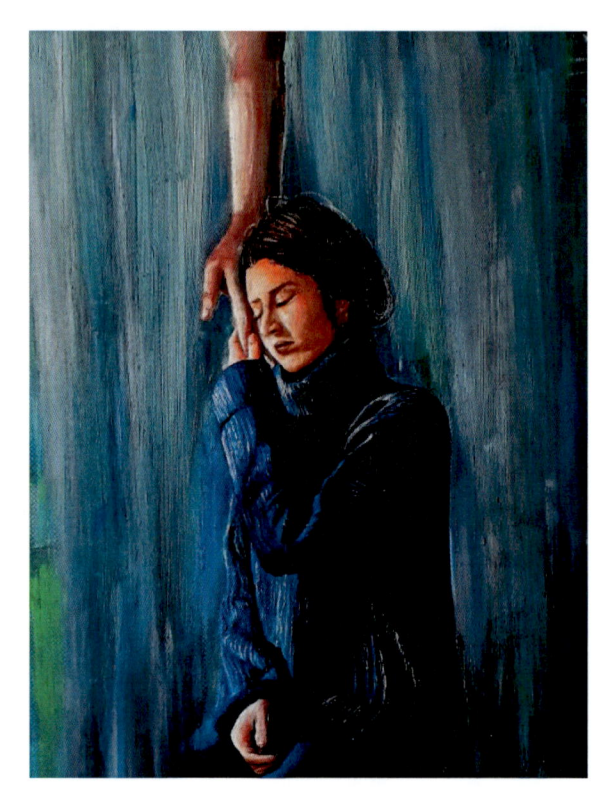

Artist Credits - © Sara Fatah Samsom
@sroo_as16

Sara Fatah Samsom was one of the first artists that allowed me to write poetry impressions of her art. I have watched her talents blossom and mature with time. Each step of her development has been exciting to witness.

Sara is a gifted, self-taught talent and a member of the "Artist Join." She is an incredible artist whose virtual gallery gives us a peek into a "Must See" world. Her unique art is mysteriously thought-provoking, primitive, emotional, and intellectual.

- JNM

A LOVE FAR AWAY

I long to hold my love
A love far away
Will not be here today
Will not be here tomorrow

A touch so perfect
Yet seems so distant
When I am all alone
Thinking about you
I long to hold my love
A love so far away

A love so deep
A love wanting to hold
A love wanting to keep
I long to hold my love
A love so far away

A touch so warm and sweet
Everything I could ever want
Nothing I could ever have

I long to hold my love
A love so far away
Will not be here today
Will not be here tomorrow

- Writer's Thoughts -

This featured piece fascinated me from the beginning. My impressions were of a longing for a love that was so far away. Everything one could ever want, but nothing that could ever be had. It's a love so far away, that will not be here today, and not be here tomorrow. Just a love so far away.

Artist Credits - © Vicki Sullivan
@0ne_flow

"As I stare out the streetcar window, I wish that maybe, just maybe you would walk up the stairs of this same streetcar see my face and just stare the way that you used to and maybe that one glance would make you fall in love with me
all over again maybe, just maybe"

—— Anonymous

STREETCAR CALLED DESIRE

A love blazes inside me today, searching for a way that our tomorrows may fuse into a gentle itch that I carry in this old weary heart of mine

Dreaming of your soft voice hearing those words as passengers on that streetcar called desire

It's with a flame that glows dusk through dawn for those wanton impulses smoldering in my soul for your sensuous touch

Those urges of mine, serving as hints each new day how much I need you more than any of those other yesterdays

It's with a weak vulnerability, that I confess these words of lust for you, with impatient desires as they glisten into this new day.

Images of your presence echo into my thoughts, wantin' to ride that streetcar called desire just one more time

Just one more time

- Writer's Thoughts -

These words of poetry were inspired loosely by Tennessee Williams' novel "Streetcar Named Desire.

Artist Credits - ©Eskander Dawani
@iskander.dawani

"No language has ever had a word for a virgin man."

—— Will Durant

THAT GIRL OF MINE

That girl of mine writing about her consumes my euphoric state of mind making me delirious with thoughts of my lost virginity through these words of poetry

When I write about her, I write with simplicity as if I was seducing her for the first time with lyrics that are smooth as vintage jazz

For you see, this girl of mine has restored that passion back into my soul, enticing these words of poetic virginity written just for her

That girl, who releases my words of ripened literary promiscuity, how I adore her so

- Writer's Thoughts -

Sometimes when I write poetry about those love things, it can feel like that time I lost my virginity. With a sensation of those words ripening as they wither untasted on the vine until they are released with literary promiscuity.

Artist Credits - ©Eskander Dawani
@iskander.dawani

"Farewells can be shattering, but returns are surely worse. Solid flesh can never live up to the bright shadow cast by its absence. Time and distance blur the edges; then suddenly the beloved has arrived, and it's noon with its merciless light, and every spot and pore and wrinkle and bristle stands clear."

—— Margaret Atwood

WAITING

I'll always wait for you
I'll be lingering right here
just waiting with expectations of a return

Even when I'm insecure that you will not come back, I'll just be waiting right here for your retrieval

Giving pause to a time that may never come, but all the same, with all my insecurities and vulnerabilities
I'll be right here, just waiting anyhow

I'll place my heart on the window seal of my soul, waiting in the warmth of a summer breeze as the gentle winds whisper, reminding me to be patient as I wait right here for your return

Struggling with my exposed inhibitions offering me doubts, I'll still be lingering right here, waiting in anticipation of your return, a time that may never come about

But all the same, I'll just be right here waiting anyhow for you to return and retrieve my heart, contemplating a day that may never come about

- Writer's Thoughts -

This piece of poetry is based loosely on reflections of my past days as a soldier. A time of just waiting with my insecure vulnerabilities for a love to return that never occurred. But all the same, I was just right there waiting anyhow for that love to return and retrieve my heart that never came about.

Artist Credits - ©Eskander Dawani
@iskander.dawani

" I think you still love me, but we can't escape the fact that I'm not enough for you. I knew this was going to happen. So I'm not blaming you for falling in love with another. I'm not angry, either. I should be, but I'm not. I just feel pain. A lot of pain. I thought I could imagine how much this would hurt, but I was wrong."

—— Haruki Murakami

WICKED SIN

A touch, so tender but yet so seductive; whispers with gentle discretion, but yet so full of wicked intentions; a moan of a euphoric surrender to those desires that fuel salacious necessities

No words will be spoken; no promises to be broken; no looking back - no regrets for a lust-filled liaison on this night of wicked sin

Longing to be as one with such precious little time; both promised to another; being lonely their only crime

In a moment of weakness, understanding that tomorrow will bring with it temporal guilt, with fading memories of this one night's infidelities

It's with no regrets on this night of wicked sin, being lonely the only crime

- Writer's Thoughts -

I once read that infidelity is the opium of unfaithfulness. Well, that explains a lot about a past partner's addition to promiscuity. That pain of infidelity never goes away, it lingers, it's just with you forever.

JUST POETRY

"You talk when you cease to be at peace with your thoughts."

—— Kahlil Gibran, The Prophet

WYETH'S INFLUENCE
(a Tanka Poem)

Artist Credits - © Khurram Amir
@khurramamir_mustdraw

An artist's tribute
Youthful interpretation
a "Faraway" sketch

Wyeth's magical influence
Captivating a young mind

- Writer's Thoughts -

Khurram Amir has captured the soul of Andrew Wyeth with his youthful interpretation of " Faraway". Simply an extraordinary tribute to a great American artist. Wyeth's magical influence clearly captivated a talented young mind for the world to witness.

Artist Credits - © Viktoriya (Vicky) Golbraykh
@vickyssketchbook

"Ya got cigarettes?" she asks.
"Yes," I say, "I got cigarettes." "Matches?" she asks.
"Enough to burn Rome." "Whiskey?"
"Enough whiskey for a Mississippi River
of pain." "You drunk?" "Not yet."

—— Charles Bukowski

DRINKIN' DURING THE DAY

Don't say you're doin just fine
Don't hide yourself away
Got something on your mind
You're drinkin during the day
Breaking from the guilt
It's alright to just hurt

Don't say that it's okay
Stop protesting the agony
Just because you hurtin
You're drinking in the day
Crumbling from the sorrow
It's alright to just cry

Don't say you're doin alright
Don't suppress yourself away
There's pain, that's on your mind
Decaying from the burden inside
It's alright to just have a good cry
Because you're drinking during the day
Frittering yourself away

- Writer's Thoughts -

Just introspections from an uncomfortable time in a past life, remembering the painful guilt of watching a spirit decay from all that drinking during the day, just trying to drown those sorrows away. Because she was just drinking during the day frittering a life away.

SELF PORTRAIT
(a Haiku)

Artist Credits - © JNM

Within every poet
Yearns a Picasso's soul
Wistful self-portrait

•

- Writer's Thoughts -

I wanted to paint a self-portrait of sorts; These words of poetry I write for you are reflections of my travels throughout life. They represent a lifetime of joy, suffering, pain, grief, anxieties, love things, and moments of peaceful solitude.

They are my way of expunging those introspections, I've carried far too long. They're simply poetry of who I once was, composed by a weary old soul.

"How can I begin anything new with all of yesterday in me?"
—— Leonard Cohen

Artist Credits © Kinga E. Vnuk
@kingavnuk

"Cotton blooms"
Pastels on UArt.
December 31st, 2021

This beautiful piece of inspiring art is from the multi-talented Artist Kinga Vnuk's collection. I encourage you to visit her Instagram Page @kingavnuk or her website at: kingaevnuk.com

You will not be disappointed.

—— JNM

COTTON BLOOMS

The garden in my past doesn't have the colors of spring, it has the feel of pointed edges of those cotton bolls blooming between my fingers, those are the days I recall, as I yearn for those white meadows vocalizing this poetry which I hold in spiritual harmony

Those glorious cotton blooms the Sakura of the South, the original sin of gardening, with an appearance of innocence breathing life into our souls

That magnificent white fluffy flower, nature's artificial snowballs blossoming into the Southern summer's heat tossed into playful exhibitions, often caught in a dancing sky amidst our imaginations

Those cotton fields, so elegantly rendered into Artist's portraits, with their hazy and languid purity, the transient pinnacles of grace promising sanguinity into our lives

Reclining in the farmer's field as if to cloak into a sea of white clouds, striking a chord that no other crop can, ripening our souls with its simple white prominence

That soft Southern Sakura breathing life into our souls, a gift of nature to be admired for its grace, respected for its storied yore

- Writer's Thoughts -

I was intrigued to learn that so many people have never seen cotton growing in a field. So, I thought I'd do a poem about it because cotton and I go way back! My Father's family were Cotton Farmers. To me, cotton is a gift of nature to be admired for its beauty but respected for its storied history.

Artist Credits - © Darya Karabchuk.
@darya_karabchuk

"That's the power you possess as an artist.
To find and express your own unique message."

—— Ella Leya,

"The Orphan Sky"

OBSESSION

Those obsessions enslaving our consciousness arousing creations through representations - you know, those obsessed illustrations of raw expositions, with drifting views of occurrences evolving into innocence often with a flair of suggestive dangerous allure, with everything in between

Those obsessions so soft as an angel's feather - but vicious as a nightmare's affliction possessing the soul cultivating with the grandeur of an illusionist

That obsession of a wild soul, the one that we don't quite understand, the one that devours our artistic desires inducing our passions, all while enslaving our consciousness

Those suppliers of our addictions, arousing creations, stories through representations - you know, those obsessed illustrations of raw expositions that we are so fond of those Artist's obsessions

- Writer's Thoughts -

In my continual search for inspiration, somehow, I always find my way back to one of my favorite artists Darya Karabchuk. Her gift for creative expression has no limits.

Just looking into Darya's eyes tells you all you need to know about her artistic obsession. Those eyes so soft as an angel's feather - but fierce as a nightmare's affliction, possessing the soul with curiousness, creation with the grandeur of an illusionist. Yes, those obsessive alluring eyes enslaving our consciousness.

Artist Credits - © Darya Karabchuk.
@darya_karabchuk

"Out of clutter, find simplicity.
From discord, find harmony.
In the middle of difficulty lies harmony.'

— Albert Einstein

TOOLS OF CREATIVITY

Those tools of creativity - out of clutter a creative elusive clarity - foreseeing patches of color and tones of possibilities, delivering artistic impressions in its simplicity

Those esoteric tools of inspiration aspired to cultivate anticipations of mastery

Those devices of modest extensions of our minds, much as the branches are to fruits of our labor

Those mystical tools of mysteries creating Picassos, Van Goghs, Wyeth's and Rembrandt's - yes, those tools of creativity - foreseeing patches of color and tones of possibilities

- Writer's Thoughts -

Writing this piece was inspired by the simplicity in which the artist seemingly creates out of clutter an elusive clarity that only they know, it's those impressions of simplicity, those mystical tools of mysteries That foreseeing patches of color and tones of possibilities.

Artists Credits - © Viktoriya (Vicky) Golbraykh
@vickyssketchbook

"Women don't endure simply because they can;
no, women endure because they aren't given any other
choice - they wanted them weak but forced them to be strong"

— Amanda Lovelace

STRONG SIMPLICITY

Strong with a simplistic refinement in an elegant way - not frail or assembled to outfit the latest rage apparel...just simply a matron of dignity with jubilant stories, of intriguing mystery

An inner beauty pursuing and weaving the ordinary into fine silk with sheer clarity

When I tell them, you are more than it seems; they think I'm telling lies that you are a woman of prestige

When I tell them, your grace rests inside your mind, your heart, your soul; not in the perceptions of you; they think I'm telling them lies that you are a woman of degree

When I tell them, that the simple things about you are the extraordinary things, that only the wise can see; they think I'm telling them lies that you are a woman of simplicity

Cause I know your loveliness - that beauty - that power that resides deep inside of you

Cause I know you are a woman refined in an elegant way, with a sense of strong simplicity - a woman of intriguing mystery that only I can see

- Writer's Thoughts -

These words of poetry were inspired Amanda Lovelace's The Witch Doesn't Burn in This One (Women Are Some Kind of Magic)
I have always admired women of great courage, grace, and strength to endure in a world dominated by men.

Artist Credits - © Eskander Dawani
@iskander.dawani

"Sadly enough, the most painful goodbyes
are the ones that are left unsaid
and never explained."

—— Jonathan Harnisch, Freak

TEARS

My heart aches with grief; painful tears pour from lifeless eyes into a sorrowful soul

No farewell words were spoken no time for good-byes
You left before I knew it. Only you know why

No matter where you are now, you'll always share that hallowed place you left behind

I know I shouldn't mourn; you would disapprove
I'd remember only the happiness that will never be anymore

I've cried those tears of hurt, wishing I had all those moments we could have shared; you know, those that I chose to ignore

My grief will be forever It will not go away It will be part of who I am step for step, breath for breath

Now all that remains is just a feeling of dreadfulness that depletes, knowing you will be nobody's sister anymore

- Writer's Thoughts -

In memory of a sister (Sheelagh Sullivan) who is now a guardian angel in heaven.

Death brings pain that time can only heal; no words can ease what we truly feel; her joy is eternally sealed and cherish her memories that death can't even steal.

Rest in peace, dear Sheelagh; you will be truly missed.

Artist Credits - © Viktoriya (Vicky) Golbraykh
@vickyssketchbook

"She sacrifices her dreams to make my dream come true."

—— Luffina Lourduraj

GIVER OF LIFE

As in a warm summer breeze, calm within the chaos, strength in blessings uttered soft and sincere, the wonder and grace of my precious mother, no one else could replace, my giver of life

With a gracious spirit and irreplaceable absolute love giving up herself and her ambitions, but not on me, not on my dreams, my giver of life

Nurturing out of wisdom and compassion, the only true tenderness we can ever find comes from a mother's bonding love, my giver of life

- Writer's Thoughts -

Viktoriya (Vicky) Golbraykh is a wonderful new artist that I discovered recently. Vicky's art is incredibly eclectic; her virtual gallery is an intriguing collection of artworks, a unique perspective full of raw emotions.

This featured piece of art, "The Journey," was one of her first drawings inspired by thoughts of her own mother. The title was selected to represent people's difficulties during exhausting migrations.

Model / Muse - © Valerie Heysen
@valerieheysen

"The grip of her eyes is so hard that he can barely breathe. She entices him to crash into her and explore her depths. But he is already soaked in different waters."

—— Faraaz Kazi

SOULFUL EYES

Those deep soulful eyes with an unblemished sense of interpretation affirming the subtleties of complexities

Virtuous eyes, too sincere to mask the precious soul ablaze behind them

Profound absorbing eyes divulging the mysteries of discretions

Orifices of darkness arousing the depths of loveliness, inferring a solemnity, all with a beauty that still resides deep inside a soul - beholding the grace of an angel

Those deep soulful eyes with a true sense of elegance, affirming the subtleties of complexities

- Writer's Thoughts -

Valerie Heysen a muse of my heart's poetic eloquence. Her confidence, so brave, so free, with a seductive gaze that absorbs my words; my elegant muse, my soliloquy!

Artist Credits - © Khurram Amir
@khurramamir_mustdraw

"Hope is the thing with feathers.
That perches in the soul
And sings the tune without the words.
And never stops - at all."

—— Emily Dickinson

KINDRED SPIRITS

No bonds are greater than sacred alliances that have endured the test of time - like feathers tightly laced together forging true kinships into divine spirituality

The sort of spirit that accepts us from the darkness of times to the luminance of hope, an essence cloaked as angels with feathered wings guiding the way

Those tightly laced feathers - the uncommon commitment of hope to preserve through adversity - it's that kindred spirit you and I deliver as we amble along the trail of tears together

That bond of our souls you and I have together - our caring alliance of hope and perseverance

- Writer's Thoughts -

At the request of my dear friend Alta H. Mabin - Haffner; I wrote this poem as a gift of hope in collaboration of " Feathers for Hena"

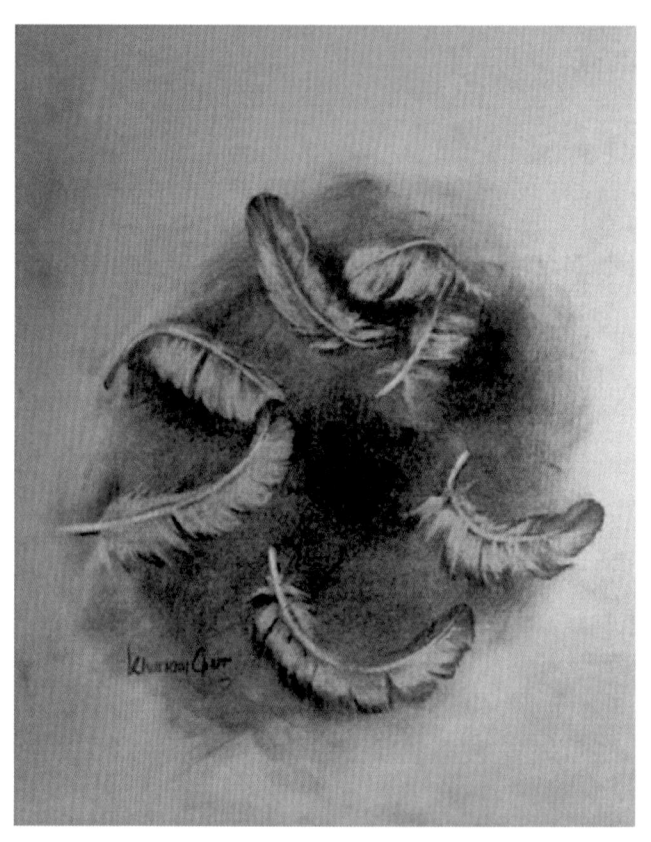

Artist Credits - © Khurram Amir
@khurramamir_mustdraw

"Trauma is personal. It does not disappear if it is not validated. When it is ignored or invalidated the silent screams continue internally heard only by the one held captive. When someone enters the pain and hears the screams healing can begin."

—— Danielle Bernock,

FALLEN ANGEL

There was a feeling, I could have been someone, I used to fly with wings

Ravages and horridness of a cruel tormented life, has broken those wings

Nothing seems to be the same as before, struggles are to countless coming way too often

Dark repressed demons always lurking in the shadows, consuming every anxiety

I plead, I beg, I implore, please harvest my soul

You see, I could have been someone, now, just a fallen soldier with imperfect wings, a one-way ticket with reservations to meet my maker

- Writer's Thoughts -

I once wrote that I scribble my thoughts to express my raw emotion; to release my introspections, to share my anguish; to expel those demons. I write with uneasiness about sharing my words for fear of opinion; I write because my story is worth sharing; I write because it is who I am; I just write, it's what I do. But in the end, I write because I am someone.

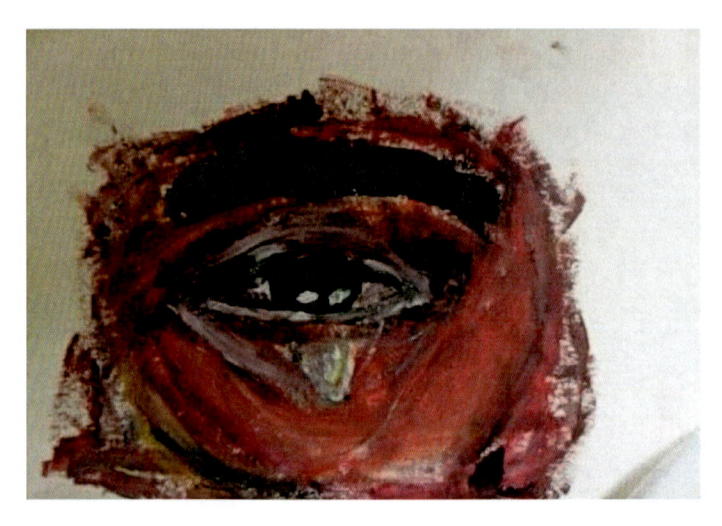

Artist Credits - © Donna M. Magsoling
Donna Marie @dawnnnaaaa

"A flower knows when its butterfly will return,
and if the moon walks out, the sky will understand;
but now it hurts to watch you leave so soon when I don't know if you
will ever come back."

—— Sanober Khan

FINALITY

Life is just another story I can't tell anymore, there is never a real ending just a place where the story seems to fade into darkness

Finalizing my list, expiring those unwritten words, wrapping up that unfinished business, it really doesn't matter what you call it; all that matters is recognizing every moment is a precious thing, arriving with it the courage of finality

So, for now, I will miss you like I'll never see you again, the next time I meet you, I will write to you like I'll never write for anyone else again

In this moment of farewell, remember me with a smile, for it's better to forget than to remember me for never having said goodbye

- Writer's Thoughts -

I left my family many decades ago, not knowing if I would ever return. Never really saying goodbye, expecting to see them again. After all these years, I know the end is near; there is no one to say goodbye to, no one interested in witnessing my finality - just no one there...

ACKNOWLEDGMENTS

Forward

Fazila Moosa is a close confidant who, through her continued support, has been one of my greatest influences on this poetic journey. This book would have never been a reality without her literary console and friendship. I am truly honored to have such an accomplished published author write this brief introduction to this book of poetry of mine.

Contributing Editor

Alta H. Mabin - Haffner has been a guiding presence on this project and in my life. Without her constant mentorship and belief in my words of poetry, I would have never had the courage to document my Travels throughout life. Alta has opened many doors to me for publication opportunities. Her vigilance and tireless efforts to guide me through this difficult process have been unparalleled. Throughout this project, she has been a mentor, coach, and above all a true friend.

Special Acknowledgement

Kerri C. Kelly- McManus, my loving, supportive Soulmate, has given me the courage to put these Travels of mine into poetry. I'm so fortunate to have her presence in my life, she nourishes and completes my soul. Without her console I truly would be a lost spirit on this Journey of mine.

Book Cover by

Donna M. Magsoling (Original Design)
Airesh Kate Caliso (Digital Enhancement)

Contributing Artist

I want to thank all the amazing artists who contributed their art to support this poetic journey of mine. Each artist has brought a unique perspective to this project. Without them, my words of poetry would be just words without artistic meaning. I am truly grateful for their presence in my literary world.

Illustrations by

Donna M. Magsoling
Airesh Kate Caliso
Emma Eevantytär
Debora Lapa
Darya Karabchuk
Erin Murphy
Kinga E. Vnuk
Khurram Amir
Subhrodwip Karmakar
Paul Quintero
Pita Nketiah
Indi Henri
Skandi Dawani
Sara Fatah Samsom
Valerie Heysen
Vicky Sullivan
Yeimei Wangsa
Rita Taha
Viktoriya (Vicky) Golbraykh

ABOUT THE AUTHOR

James (Jim) McManus

Jim is a poet from a small village by the Sea in Rhode Island. He has garnered much acclaim for his work abroad as a Humanitarian, building critical infrastructure in impoverished areas worldwide. Pulling from those experiences and life's sometimes cruelties, Jim shapes those memories into poetry for others to bear witness.

Jim's poetry reflects his travels throughout life. They represent a lifetime of joy, pain, suffering, grief, anxieties, love things, and moments of peaceful solitude. It is his way of expunging those introspections that have been carried as baggage for far too long.

Jim posts his work on Instagram, @s.j.beaux; he has appeared in several anthologies (Our Seasons of Syllables, Hope is a Group Project, and Feathers for Hena) and has been featured on "Poets Unlimited" and "Grief Magazine" as a new upcoming poet of interest.

Made in United States
North Haven, CT
16 September 2023